Meerkat's Burrow

by Dee Phillips

Consultants:

Dr. Alex Thornton
BBSRC David Phillips Research Fellow, Centre for Ecology and Conservation, University of Exeter, Exeter, UK

Kimberly Brenneman, PhD
National Institute for Early Education Research, Rutgers University, New Brunswick, New Jersey

New York, New York

Credits

Cover, © Jean-François Ducasse/age fotostock/Superstock and © Mark Newman/FLPA; 2–3, © Pyshnyy Maxim Vjacheslavovich/Shutterstock; 4–5, © Vincent Grafhorst/Minden Pictures/FLPA; 7T, © LianeM/Shutterstock; 7B, © Mixrinho/Shutterstock; 8–9, © Nigel Dennis Wildlife Photography; 10, © Jearu/Shutterstock; 11, © Aaron Amat/Shutterstock, © Dean Bertoncelj/Shutterstock, © tratong/Shutterstock, and © Tina Rencelj/Shutterstock; 12, © Richard Du Toit/Nature Picture Library; 13, © L. Kennedy/Alamy; 14–15, © Ecoprint/Shutterstock, and © Stu Porter/Shutterstock; 14B, © Johan Swanepoel/Shutterstock; 15, © DragoNika/Shutterstock and © Aaron Amat/Shutterstock; 16, © Edgar Thissen/PG Photography; 17, © Biosphoto/Superstock; 18, © David Curl/Nature Picture Library; 19, © Mark Newman/FLPA; 20, © mylifeiscamp/Shutterstock; 21, © Thomas Dressler/Ardea; 22, © Stu Porter/Shutterstock, © Aaron Amat/Shutterstock, © mylifeiscamp/Shutterstock, © Pyshnyy Maxim Vjacheslavovich/Shutterstock, © Richard Du Toit/Nature Picture Library, and © Henk Bentiage/Shutterstock; 23TL, © Dean Bertoncelj/Shutterstock; 23TC, © iStockphoto/Thinkstock; 23TR, © Anat Chant/Shutterstock; 23BL, © Mark Newman/FLPA; 23BC, © Johan Swanepoel/Shutterstock; 23BR, © Nigel Dennis Wildlife Photography.

Publisher: Kenn Goin
Editor: Jessica Rudolph
Creative Director: Spencer Brinker
Design: Emma Randall
Photo Researcher: Ruby Tuesday Books Ltd

Library of Congress Cataloging-in-Publication Data

Phillips, Dee, 1967– author.
Meerkat's burrow / by Dee Phillips.
pages cm. — (The hole truth! : underground animal life)
Includes bibliographical references and index.
ISBN 978-1-62724-092-5 (library binding) — ISBN 1-62724-092-6 (library binding)
1. Meerkat—Behavior—Juvenile literature. 2. Meerkat—Habitat—Juvenile literature. I. Title.
II. Series: Phillips, Dee, 1967– Hole truth!
QL737.C235P46 2014
599.74'2—dc23
2013036957

For more information, write to Bearport Publishing Company, Inc., 45 West 21st Street, Suite 3B, New York, New York 10010. Printed in the United States of America.

10 9 8 7 6 5 4 3 2 1

A Meerkat's Home 4
Check Out a Meerkat 6
Meet a Meerkat Mob 8
Welcome to a Meerkat's Burrow 10
Digging for Dinner 12
Staying Safe from Enemies 14
A Burrow for Babies 16
Leaving the Burrow 18
Learning to Be a Meerkat 20

Science Lab 22
Science Words 23
Index 24
Read More 24
Learn More Online 24
About the Author 24

A Meerkat's Home

It's morning in a **desert** in Africa.

Suddenly, a furry meerkat peeks out of a hole in the sandy ground.

The little creature makes sure no enemies are nearby.

Then it leaves its **burrow**.

Soon, other members of the meerkat family dart out of their underground home.

How would you describe a meerkat to someone who has never seen one?

Meerkats sleep, raise their babies, and stay safe from enemies in their burrows.
burrow
a meerkat family

Check Out a Meerkat

Meerkats are small animals that have tan and gray fur with dark bands across their backs.

An adult meerkat is about ten inches (25 cm) long.

It weighs less than two pounds (907 g)—about as much as a large squirrel.

Meerkats make their homes in hot deserts in southern Africa.

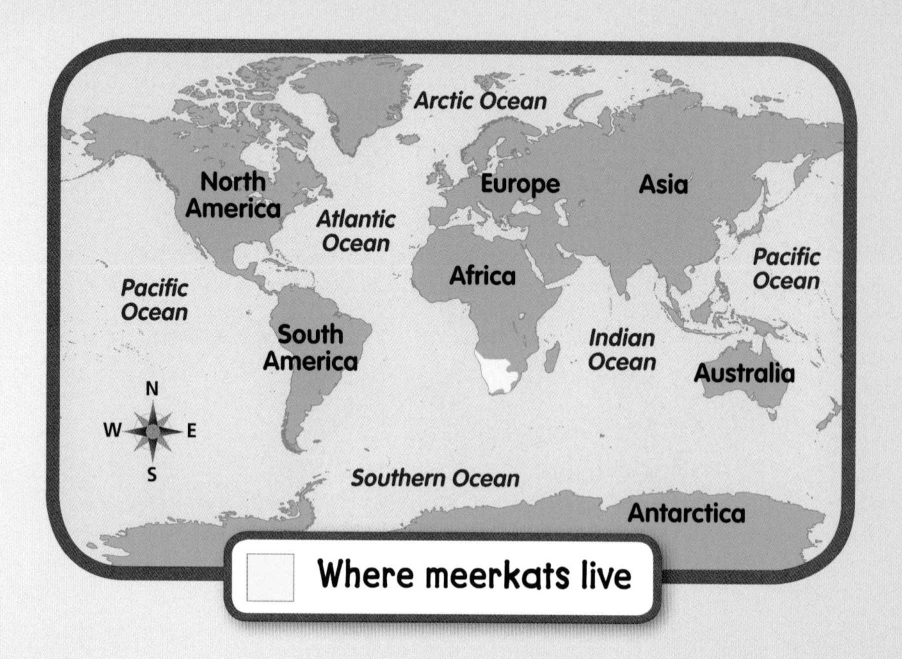

Where meerkats live

Meerkats are not actually a type of cat. They belong to a family of small, meat-eating animals called mongooses.

How do meerkats and yellow mongooses look the same? How do they look different?

Meet a Meerkat Mob

Meerkats live in groups called mobs.

Each mob has about 20 to 50 members.

The group is led by a male and a female leader.

The other meerkats are usually the leaders' sons and daughters.

All the members of a mob live together in a burrow.

A mob might have as many as 20 burrows in the area where it lives, called a **territory**. The mob lives in one burrow for a few days. Then it moves to a different burrow to search for food in a new area.

A meerkat's burrow is made up of small rooms connected by tunnels. What do you think the rooms are used for?

Welcome to a Meerkat's Burrow

Meerkats often dig their own burrows.

Sometimes, they use burrows built by other animals, such as ground squirrels.

After the other animals move out, the meerkats take over.

Then the meerkat family adds new parts to their home.

They use their long claws to dig new holes for going in and out.

They dig more underground tunnels and small rooms, too.

Meerkats don't use their claws only to dig burrows. What else might they use their claws for?

burrow entrance
burrow entrance
burrow entrance
bedroom
tunnels
bedroom
bathroom
bedroom
Some rooms in a burrow are used for sleeping, while others are used for going to the bathroom.

Digging for Dinner

At night, a meerkat mob sleeps in one of the family's burrows.

When morning comes, the family leaves the burrow to look for food.

Meerkats eat **insects**, scorpions, spiders, lizards, snakes, small birds, and eggs.

Meerkats sniff the ground to find some small animals hidden under the sand.

Then they quickly dig up tasty meals with their long claws.

a meerkat digging for food

Scorpions can harm and even kill other animals by stinging them with their tails. A meerkat will avoid getting stung by quickly biting off a scorpion's tail before eating it.
scorpion

Staying Safe from Enemies

Meerkats have many enemies, including eagles and wild dogs called jackals.

To stay safe, meerkats dig special tunnels called bolt holes.

When a mob is looking for food, one meerkat acts as a guard.

The guard stands on a rock and watches for **predators**.

If it spots one, the guard barks or whistles a warning call.

Then the meerkats dive underground into their bolt holes.

A meerkat mob may dig up to 2,000 bolt holes in its territory! A bolt hole may be up to three feet (0.9 m) deep.

A Burrow for Babies

A few times each year, a mob's two leaders **mate**.

About ten weeks later, the female gives birth to three or four tiny pups.

The meerkat pups are born in the burrow.

The mother meerkat feeds the tiny pups with milk from her body.

Each day, a mother meerkat leaves the burrow to find food for herself. While she is gone, another adult meerkat watches over the pups.

a mother meerkat carrying a pup

A newborn baby meerkat weighs about one ounce (28 g). Hold five quarters in your hand. The coins weigh about the same as a baby meerkat.

Leaving the Burrow

When the pups are about three weeks old, they start to explore outside their home.

At first, the pups play near the burrow while an adult watches over them.

At four weeks old, they start to look for food with the rest of the group.

The baby meerkats still drink their mother's milk, though, until they are about four months old.

a meerkat pup eating a lizard

Meerkat pups follow adults to learn where to find food. Adults catch food and give it to the pups to eat.

Meerkat pups must learn what foods to eat. What other things do you think pups need to learn as they grow up?

Learning to Be a Meerkat

Adult meerkats teach pups how to hunt by bringing them live animals to chase.

The pups also learn to run to a bolt hole when they hear a warning call.

At one year old, meerkats are ready to take their turns at being a guard.

They also help watch over their mother's new pups.

The young meerkats are now adult members of the mob.

Some adult meerkats stay with their parents' mob. Others leave their family to become leaders of new mobs.

Science Lab

Meerkat Life

Think about what's going on in the picture below. Then, on small pieces of paper, copy the labels to the right. Place the labels over the correct parts of the picture.

bedroom | predator | burrow entrance

bolt hole | guard | digging meerkat

(The answers are on page 24.)

Science Words

burrow (BUR-oh) a hole or tunnel dug by an animal to live in

desert (DEZ-urt) dry land with few plants and little rainfall; deserts are often covered with sand

insects (IN-sekts) small animals that have six legs, three main body parts, and a hard covering

mate (MAYT) to come together in order to have young

predators (PRED-uh-turz) animals that hunt and eat other animals

territory (TER-uh-tor-ee) the area where an animal lives and finds its food

Index

Africa 4, 6
bolt holes 14–15, 20, 22
burrows 4–5, 8–9, 10–11, 12, 16–17, 18, 22
claws 10, 12
deserts 4, 6
digging 10, 12, 14–15, 22
enemies 4–5, 14–15, 22
food 8, 12–13, 14, 16, 18–19
guards 14–15, 20, 22
mating 16
mobs 8–9, 12, 14–15, 16, 20–21, 22
mongooses 6–7
mother meerkats 16–17, 18–19, 20
pups 5, 16–17, 18–19, 20
scorpions 12–13
size 6, 17
sleeping 5, 11, 12
territories 8, 15

Read More

Harasymiw, Therese. *Meerkats (Animals That Live in the Grasslands)*. New York: Gareth Stevens (2011).

Marsh, Laura. *Meerkats (National Geographic Readers)*. Washington, D.C.: National Geographic (2013).

Schuetz, Kari. *Meerkats (Blastoff! Readers: Animal Safari)*. Minneapolis, MN: Bellwether Media (2012).

Learn More Online

To learn more about meerkats, visit
www.bearportpublishing.com/TheHoleTruth!

About the Author

Dee Phillips lives near the ocean on the southwest coast of England. She develops and writes nonfiction and fiction books for children of all ages.

Answers

Answers to the activity on page 22.